SEASONS
of the SOUL

38 Lyric Poems

BEVERLEY MANLEY

EPIGRAPH

Edward Frank Allen

Today poetry is an absolute necessity. The world needs it for its vitalizing strength. Poetry came into being because of this need, and it is perpetuated for the same reason.

… It satisfies a hunger for beauty that is a part of nearly every normal person's make-up.

It recaptures vanished moments and recreates things that have grown dim through passing years.

DEDICATION

This book is dedicated to all my friends at the Black Cat Poets
here in Truth or Consequences, New Mexico,
who have supported and encouraged my poetry.

FOREWORD

A dozen years ago in the arid mountains of northern New Mexico, at a retreat center overseen by the Virgin Mary – her sculpture adorned the retreat center entrée – I met a remarkable, delightful woman who was unlike anyone who'd attended my workshops before. Beverley Manley, who asked that I call her Bev, possessed the extreme vitality, ardent curiosity, emotional intensity, and determination to live every moment to its fullest that I've come to recognize as marks of the poet-seeker, the visionary, the wise outsider looking in. I will never forget her recital of the poem "Manxie Cat" for our group at the Mandala Center, or Bev's genius for captivating the room, hamming it up for our rapturous cohort. When the reading was over, she bowed from the waist with tears in her eyes, a startled smile lighting up her lovely face.

We stayed in touch over the years, Bev and I, then began to speak more frequently when she asked me to guide her through the writing of a book. We talked long-distance about her memoir-in-progress, her spiritual essays, but especially about Bev's poetry, which was always the closest thing to her heart, from our homes in New Mexico and New York. The poetry anthology quickly took precedence, with Bev reciting pieces to me over the phone, and me offering advice on how to separate the wheat from the chaff. She carefully considered my comments, tossed the juvenilia and lesser poems into a drawer, and polished to a sheen the 38 poems in this volume before sending them off to the publisher.

All true writing comes at a cost. Beverley Manley's work matters precisely because it's been hard-earned and gestated from in her depths, drawing power from severe childhood trauma, agonizing parental loss, forbidden love, and the ordeals of being a freethinking, sexual, irreverent female in a society oppressed by the glaring male gaze. These poems speak of Bev's losses, her encounters with the sublime, her lust, love of nature and language, as well as the wounds to justice, equality, and freedom she has witnessed over a long and eventful lifetime.

Like a majority of working artists, Bev has earned a living doing jobs that have nothing to do with her passions, guarding her inner life like a treasure house. She has turned to the written page as a source of beauty and intensity, a sanctuary for self-expression (off the record), and place to find her footing, and return to her center, when life buffeted her with heartbreak. The poems about forbidden love are among Bev's finest, and those written in the key of transcendence (my favorite note on her scale as a writer) are light as a feather, shot through with wonder, hard-headed – she is nobody's spiritual fool – and full of gratitude for the miraculous life unfolding before her.

It has been my true joy and honor to help Bev in assembling this book of poems, and bring her singular, lyrical voice into the world. I hope that these poems assist you in greeting the day, standing a bit taller, asking tougher questions, dancing more, paying deeper attention to the sunrise, and bringing an increase of love and care into this baffling, wonderful world.

Mark Matousek
Springs, New York
December, 2022

INTRODUCTION TO
SEASONS OF THE SOUL –
38 POEMS BY BEVERLEY MANLEY

I wrote these poems over the span of my life with no thought of collecting them into a book. Some experiences were so powerful that they prompted me to strive to write a poem that would make them live as long as the poem lived. It could have been a scene, a mood, an emotion, an insight, a spiritual experience, or a story. I also wrote to vent the rage I felt when my indigenous friends described the injustices endured in boarding schools – deep wounds that sometimes would never be healed.

The year of my birth was 1935. The place was Independence, Missouri in the Heartland of America. The Dust Bowl and the Great Depression were in full swing along with Prohibition. Kansas City with its warring criminal gangs added a sense of danger and drama which stirred the dramatic flare in me.

An early memory is my mother cuddling me almost daily on the couch to read me poems and stories. She had the patience to help me memorize whatever poem I wanted. This she did from the time I was two until her death when I was seven.

During this time her father, who came from Germany as an adult, lived with us. He would lift me to his lap to tell me stories of his homeland, stories of the Black Forest, and the Lorelei singing on her rock in the River Rhine. He cuddled me close and sang so sweetly in his native tongue that music and poems and stories poetically told became entwined in my mind and soul forevermore – making me the poet and storyteller I have always been.

Were it not for my mother and my grandfather, would I even be a poet?

My mother's reading to me was our main way of sharing love. We didn't talk about personal things. In fact, no one in our family did. I thought it was strange, though I had no other family to compare ourselves to.

One drear winter day, I think I was five and my sister June was thirteen, Mamma made us sit on the couch so she could tell us something "necessary to know."

She began with, "You must always be stoic." "What's that?" I wanted to know. "Stoic means never showing your feelings. Keeping your face like a closed book with no pictures or title on the cover. Never tell anyone what you're feeling. Never share your desires, dreams, goals, or loves, because the better someone knows you the more power they have to hurt you. The ideal is to die with no one having known you. "

My stomach lurched at her last thought. It sickened my very soul. NO! NEVER! For me, a life lived like that would not *be* a life.

Now I knew why the six of us never said anything personal at the supper table. I knew why there was no fighting, only an occasional stiff, cold, jagged silence or thick tension in the air. Saddest of all, I never once saw any sign of affection between Mamma and Daddy. The various atmospheres in our home fueled my poems for years to come.

Up until Mamma's unexpected death when I was seven, my need for genuine heart-to-heart connection grew painfully, energizing my drive to turn my feelings into a form of art – my first being classical piano which I studied for seven years.

Going back to when I was five, Mamma decided quite suddenly that I would start first grade *right then* and not wait until I was six. This was because I asked too many questions and begged her to teach me to read. This hasty decision brought to pass a dreadful scene that contributed greatly to my sense of *not* belonging.

Minutes after Mamma left me in Miss Broadway's care, I found this teacher to be either just plain mean or lacking in common sense. She pointed at me exclaiming, "You are the tallest first grader I have ever seen!" Then, pointing at a very tall boy, said "Come here, boy. Stand with your back to hers." He came. "Look, class, she's a full head taller than he is and this boy is a head taller than the next tallest boy." The kids had ample time to stare at the over-thick, long, black hair on my skinny legs.

This shaming encouraged the bully in them. For three years, till I moved to a different school, too many of them threw sticks and stones at me and called me names that hurt worse than the stones. They pushed me in mud puddles and sicced their dogs on me. But I never once thought of not going to school. There was fire in my belly for education.

Deeper in my soul was fire for happiness itself. And right then happiness meant education. As the teacher added her abuse to that of the kids, I felt anger, not self pity. I did not feel like some poor little soul who deserved it. I knew I didn't deserve it. During first grade I learned something far more important than numbers and the alphabet. I learned that I could choose my response and that my response affected my happiness right then and in the future. Knowing this made me feel free, like a bird flying over what once were barriers.

What does this have to do with generating poems? Experiencing my power to help direct my path in life kept the inner fires alive because I knew I could always do something, and that meant passion

– passion to pour into poems. Had I felt victimized, helpless, and hopeless, I would not have had the energy or the desire to write.

In second grade I learned another life-changing lesson that was not in the curriculum. It began with a choice the school had made – a choice I took advantage of. They hired a Negro lady to wash the little glass milk bottles that every student used each day. ("Negro" was the polite word back then.) I asked her to let me help her wash the bottles. "Oh, no, honey," she replied. "Go out and play with your friends." When she heard how they treated me, she gladly accepted my offer.

We conversed about all manner of things. The more we talked the more I saw that she was *not* inferior. Jim Crow teachings were lies – brutal, wicked lies – and sadly, Independence was a strongly Jim Crow Town, the worst in Missouri I've been told. That meant I was an alien in the town of my birth. More alone than ever. I cried softly into my pillow at night because I could not change the mind of my Jim Crow mother who simply closed her mind to logic.

It was clear to me that all people of color were equal to us and I wanted to help them. So when I moved to San Francisco in 1966, I took advantage of the chance to work with Native Americans. It was with them that I found my religion, close friends, and best of all, found the second of my three great romantic loves – the first having been my husband of fifteen years, Ted Manley.

Raymond Hunt, an Acoma Pueblo tribal elder and traditional drum maker who I met at Intertribal Friendship House in Oakland, formally adopted me as his daughter and named me Moonflower for "one who blooms in darkness." Poetry flowered out of this rich Native soil and it's amazing to think that this evolutionary path started with little glass milk bottles and a wise, loving African American lady in a Jim Crow Town almost eighty years ago.

After following that story to its natural conclusion it's a bit of a whiplash to return to when I was nine, but we must.

Daddy remarried, exactly one year after Mamma died, to a woman with severe personality disorders – after which came ten years of a *Hell* that I could not even imagine until I experienced it. I turned my suffering into poetry – poetry that molders away in some landfill today.

During those ten years, using beauty and love (nature, music, and dancing) as the way to having moments of real living, I came to understand that beauty and love would always be the engine, the spiritual *Way* in which I would live, love, dream, and create.

Indeed, art, the very soul of art before it takes a particular form, became the number one thing of importance in those ten years. It's doubtful I could have survived without it. The line, "My head is bloody but unbowed," from the poem "Invictus," became the mantra that kept me going. And when I was alone I reveled in classical music and danced barefoot among bright yellow *dandylions* – twirling, pointing a toe skyward, lifting my arms to the heavens.

When I was nine my parents decided it was a sin to eat the flesh of warm-blooded animals in warm weather. This meant FISH. Daddy had to feed a family of four and, bless his heart, he quickly excelled at hauling them in.

Lake Jacomo was close to Independence. In my mind's eye I can still see its shimmering surface surrounded by dense, green forest, no housing development yet. Daddy trolled or ran his overnight lines while I rowed as silently as I could – no chattering, no radio. Ah! The smooth glide was like flow in poetry. The barely audible liquid sound of the oars, like cadence. The evenly-spaced little eddies in the water, like verses of poems.

Ten years of rowing, from age nine to nineteen, left this kaleidoscope of sensations deep in my very blood and bones, giving me a need to write poetry simply for the feel of writing poetry.

From the time I began earning my own living at age 17, I preferred crunching numbers to managing people. The advantage of this choice was that it gave me *myself*. When I left the office I left my job behind, and in San Francisco that meant more things to explore and to participate in. Yes, *participate*, because I had become head-turning attractive and people reached out to me, doors opened. I belonged. My husband and I reveled in concerts, ballet, art galleries, and museums. We took long hikes through Coast Redwoods, danced rock and roll, and so much more! All rich soil for poetry (and compost too). We lived across the street from the Pacific. From our window we watched the waves roll in and felt them. They sang us to sleep. We heard ships talking in the night and the Pacific inserted itself into my poetry; "Summer Solstice" is one example.

Yes indeed, San Francisco meant change, especially cultural. Drinking it in changed me in almost every way. Now I could jump up when the mood was getting ugly on a blocked streetcar, invite a hippy guitarist to play, and soon there would be singing, clapping, and dancing. I was able to dance at Eitos Taverna and join the Pow-Wow Indians.

What absolutely did *not* change was the understanding that I was responsible for *myself*, just as everyone else was responsible for *themselves*.

It would be enriching, my readers, if you and I could know one another, but of course we can't. It seems fitting, then, that I tell you something about the seasons and the soil out of which a few of my poems germinated.

Almost assuredly, many of my poems are about things we all can relate to. "Silence" and "Quiet" come to mind. It's my hope that these poems bring sweet memories of your own, memories that bring some of that sweetness – renewed and refreshed – into your own relationships. And if you, too, use words as your primary form of artistic expression, may the first two poems in this book enliven your own search for that one perfect word. Perhaps "Why I Read Fiction" will deepen your insight and sharpen your appreciation for the value of fiction.

In San Franciso of '66 we were invited to rethink everything we thought we knew and thus I found an American form of Buddhism, studied avidly, joined a sangha, and am Buddhist to this day. It blends well with my ideas on Indigenous spirituality. Seven poems speak of this. ("The Past is Not Past," "Untitled," "The Blessing Too Often Avoided," "Caballo Lake State Park," "Revelation," "Rebirth Beside the Atlantic," and "The Ageless One.")

When I divorced and moved across the Bay to San Leandro I found my second great love. Six of my poems are about him. ("In Your Presence," "The Ageless One," "More Than One Man," "Desolation," "My Man of the Northwoods," and "So Radiant Your Humor.")

I wrote "Precious Man So Far From Me" to the man I carry in my heart today. His name could likely be my last word.

Mine is a dancing soul. If I were to lose my legs, my soul would continue to dance. Two poems here honor dancing and dancers: "To Philip, a Greek Dancer at Eitos Taverna" and "Dancing Greek at Eitos Taverna." Oh, how I delighted in the dancing itself, though not in the lifestyle I explored. That lifestyle was totally foreign to my romantic nature – which is to deeply love, honor, and admire *one* man.

One cold, windy Valentine's Day in 2009, George Loftus and I were wed on the banks of the Rio Grande. It was for George I wrote "My Fourth of July, 2015" while he was out of town. Every time I read the poem in public, he would cry. After he died in 2020, I wrote "My Heart Cannot Let Go."

Lastly, this high Chihuahuan desert in which I live never ceases to thrill me. Almost daily I stand on a high ridge and gaze in awe at ranges of mountains stretching for fifty miles; mountains continually shape-changing beneath the moving shadows of clouds. And for me, our quickly changing wild weather is the very breath of this living desert. Two poems, "March 25, 1994" and "Someday" speak of my love for this enchanted land.

The time has come to wrap this up and tie it together by emphasizing what I think is the most potent source of lyric poetry . . .

Love! Yes, love! All types of love, be it love for friends and family or such things as moonrise over snowy mountains. Yet Romantic Love, mysterious and profound, is the greatest source for me. Not all of us need or want Romantic Love, but those of us who *do* know that beautiful things become even more beautiful when we're in love. Myriad songs and poems over the centuries attest to this. And that enhanced beauty calls us to write poems about it. That's true for me. So I'm blessed to have Romantic Love given to me in my old age.

There have been three great loves in my life, each one a powerfully life-changing season for me. In each of those seasons I've grown in knowledge and wisdom, in appreciation of arts new to me, and in my own artistic ability and accomplishment.

This new love is the very pinnacle, the crown jewel, of my loves. This one is the most passionately tender and sweet, the most sacred and holy and life-renewing – even age-erasing! This new season of my long life is not the winding down it could have been. It's Spring! Joyous, creative energy fills me. Exciting possibilities are opening up. New flowers are blooming. And I love my beautiful, cherished friends even more than before. Tender premonitions hint at something wonderful.

ACKNOWLEGEMENTS

This book could not have been created without the spiritual and material help of many friends here in this small, rural, desert community with the odd name of Truth or Consequences, New Mexico.

Wendy Nine, Rebecca Otero, Mary Kinninger Walker, and Lee Sonne gave me love and moral support (as well as a little critique now and then). I love you ladies with all my heart.

George Loftus III, my recent husband, dreamed of a community of poets that would encourage one another to write and to nurture their talents without judgments voiced from their fellow poets. Working hard to realize this dream, he created *Black Cat Poets* and this is where I first met him.

We had good reason for calling ourselves by that somewhat unusual name for a community of poets, as Rhonda Britain and her husband Jay opened a store named "Black Cat Books and Coffee." Their dream was to encourage local poets. They gave us more than a home for many years, bringing in published authors for book signings and an occasional workshop. In addition, we were allowed to have our own public readings and book signings. Rhonda and Jay, I bow to you in gratitude for giving us birth and helping us shine.

Upon joining this community I quite regularly wrote a new poem each month. The writings of my fellow poets inspired me to seek and find unique subject matter. Special thanks to the staff at KRWG-TV, the PBS station for Southern New Mexico and West Texas, for always bringing the most fruitful fields for that search.

Heartfelt thanks go to Ingo Hoeppner for opening his Art Cafe to us when our former home was sold.

My friend and professional photographer, Will Quinn, took the portrait intended for the cover. But when he saw the photo of me dancing at the Old Time Fiddler's Playhouse, he exclaimed *"That's the picture that belongs on the cover! Put mine on the back."* Thanks, Will, you were right.

Undying gratitude to my friend, Carol Borsello. She was of great help with navigating the computer and setting up needed people connections, as well as a few editing suggestions along the way. She typed all 38 poems and sent them to Mark Matousek, my editor, for comments or approval. She also handled the rewrites with great patience.

Some months ago Carol left this land of russet and brown for a land of green and sparkling blue waters. In her place, like a miracle, came a lady from a place of green and many waters to this brown desert town. Mary Murray came to me just as I was starting the introduction for this book – which was, for this poet, the most difficult writing challenge ever confronted. In her capable hands I no longer felt like a babe lost in the woods. She is also responsible for the photo on my book cover. Bless you, Mary. I could not have completed this work without you. And thank you, also, for typing – and *liking* it.

A very special thank-you goes to Mark Matousek, my mentor and editor. Without him this book would surely not exist.

In July of 2013, I was seventy-seven and despairing of finding my life's purpose. I felt that I was failing to live the life that was in me to live, so eagerly joined Mark's in-person workshop called "Finding Your Genius." This incredible man actually found *mine* by bringing light into deep shadow, confirming that I was a true writer of prose and poetry, not just someone who penned a poem now and then. For the last nine years Mark has been my spiritual teacher and guide – one of the most important people in my life. I have taken his workshops and classes in person and on the internet. His books have opened my eyes and my heart; some I've read multiple times. He mentored me as I worked on a memoir and again when I turned to writing a novella. Both projects were abandoned after a *eureka moment* when I knew in my very bones that what I really wanted was to gather these poems from their hiding places and assemble them into a book. Some poems, but not all, needed editing suggestions. Within two years, during which Carol Borsello was indispensable to us, we had thirty-eight. At my request Mark put them into order, which demonstrated that the ordering of poems is an art as surely as the writing of them.

Mark, I can never thank you enough.

Beverley Manley

Contents

IN YOUR PRESENCE

To be near you is to absorb more and more
of your wordless knowledge,
Vital things no tongue can utter and no mind can analyze,
These wondrous things that make of life
a celebration and a song forever.

FEASTING ON WORDS – 1

(Stream of Consciousness)

Empty paper, invite me to revel in words –
To let them roll out from the tip of my pen –
To let them float in like gossamer
on summer zephyrs –
Float, drift, shimmer in the sun –
Languid and lazy – bringing new life.
Words come – feed me – replenish – refresh –

Refresh like cool water drawn from a deep
well in the noontide of a harvest day.
Words that squirt sweet juice in the mouth as
plums picked ripe from the tree do,
as grapes from the vine.
Words – words come fragrant and sweet
And crisp as loaves fresh from the brick oven –
As leavened bread rich with milk and eggs.
Words old and ripe as cheese
or fresh and frothy as milk squirted in a wooden pail.
Words enrich me –
Words from darkness, from light, from shadow.
Words.

June 13, 1991
Kittery, Maine

FEASTING ON WORDS – 2

(A Poem)

Words.
Wondrous words.
I love words that rouse my senses.
That whet my tongue like heady wine.
That squirt sweet juice in my mouth like a ripened plum.
Or that rouse my appetite as the scent of fresh-baked bread does.
I love words that envelop me with scents of
desert rain or of misty spruce forests.
I love words that warm my heart like embers glowing on the hearth
Or that pierce it like a lone kitten's cry.
I love words expansive as all-embracing sky, yet I also love them
Crisp and precise.
Precious words, my tools and playthings and soaring wings.
Words.

June 26, 2021

WHY I READ FICTION

I read to step outside my skin and place myself in another's.
I read to see, hear, taste, feel what they have known.
I want distant others to feel like kin.

I read to share the joy of a wife in ancient Rome
when her husband's frame fills the door.
Home at last from the Punic Wars –
Retired with pension – Free!

I need to feel the weight of sorrows I have not borne,
To know the anguish of not knowing if one's mate
be living or dying in some muddy trench.
How does one sip morning tea
then wash the china cup
and place it on the shelf,
then board the train to London
as though life were normal and nothing else?
How? Exactly how?

Yes, I read to learn how common folk rise to uncommon challenges.
Human grit, courage and will facing crushing odds.
Love and tenderness and grace that refuse to be broken.
I grow wiser, kinder, less judgmental.
I read to open my heart, my eyes, my mind.
I read to feel connection with all mankind.

September 15, 2021

SILENCE

There's mainly silence in me tonight
and I'd like to share it.
But how is that done with words?
There's various kinds of silence;
it's not empty like blank paper.
Some silence is cold and stark and hollow
Like a deserted farmhouse in December.
Some is all sharp angles in uneasy
juxtaposition – jagged lines in
black and white.
But none of that is mine tonight.

No, my silence is deep, warm & furry
Like a long-haired cat.
It's soft as pale cornsilk
Or pussy willows by the door.

My silence purrs by the hearth
Of my husband's presence.
It's serenity and safety by his side.
My silence is fulfillment –
No needs clamoring
No urgent questions.
I abide in the palpable peace of his presence –
A calm glowing gold-like embers
Soft – warm silence.

QUIET

Quiet now.
How softly rain falls on the streets of the city.
Runs in rivulets through cobblestones of burnt clay.

You and I sharing one umbrella – walking
Walking through rain gently falling –
Falling without wind or force –
Like a dream of rain – falling.
Quiet now.

All sounds muffled by enveloping mist.
A distant foghorn sounds in the channel.
Faint answer from a ship at sea.
Quiet now.

We move as one past street lights
Stretching in a line to the distance
Quaint old lights of a bygone era –

Yellowish globes in ornate wrought iron.
Each one haloed pink and green
In thickening fog,
A pearly fog chill to the cheeks –
Sweet in the nostrils.
Once again the foghorn, faint and far away
In the soft rain night –

In the empty night with only you and me
Quiet now.
Quiet.

THE PAST IS NOT PAST

The past is not past.

So say teachers I revere:
The past is not past they maintain,
It lives today,
Shapes and colors today.
Helps to make us who we are.
This is the common refrain.

It's romantic to know we're stardust
From some primal supernova,
And that our cells are awash
With ancient seas.
It's awesome that the spark of life in us
First sparked in those primal waters,
And those one-celled beings, gender non-existent,

Evolved two ways of living
Essential now for all that be,
More chose to co-operate, fewer to compete.
Vital knowledge for some say
Dog eat dog is the only way.
Yes, that knowledge can set us free of strife,

If we embrace it throughout life.
Nations clash with nations.
Some fear and distrust.
No matter where we dwell,
It's impacting all of us.

Brother can't recognize brother,
Nor sister, sister.

Trace the roots of discord down.
Where did it begin?
See how it continues now.
As understanding dawns,
Begin to make amends.

And how about me and you?
The same principle holds true,
But with a special blessing.
You see, the child is closer to the divine,
And that child lives in every breast,
In every mind.
So let's embrace that child and open to the source

As we did then.
Divine contact need not end.

There's but one life to which we all belong.
In mind and heart I feel it strong.
There's but one eternal moment
Reaching from the birth of stars to now.

To oneness my head I bow.

March 7, 2021

UNTITLED

Tree friends – teachers – mentors
Swaying – O'so slowly swaying trunks
Gracefully nodding branches soft with needles
Balancing – no effort – balancing
Not trying – just being – allowing
No resistance, but a natural grounding
Equally a friend to gravity – to air
A friend to sunlight – to darkness
Knowing the stars, the planets, the eternal cycles.
Trees firmly rooted without clinging
I am your disciple.

In Kittery, Maine 1992

REBIRTH BESIDE THE ATLANTIC –
1992

Standing in Maine woods
I lift my arms to the sky.
"Winds, blow through me.
Carry the chaff away.
Sprinkle it in the sounding sea.
I release – I release.
Clean and pure I stand.
Ready to endure the trials ahead.
Ready to grow into who I am meant to be.
I release my need to be ill, to suffer, to fear.
Oh, wind, take it all.
I'm ready to be free."

Kittery, Maine

THE BLESSING TOO
OFTEN AVOIDED

In quiet is preservation of the soul,
a portal to the Sacred Whole
in quiet the rejuvenation of body,
the creative spark of mind.
In quiet we open to blessing.
We open to the Source.
Keenly aware of oneness –
Feeling it in mind and blood and bone,
We return to daily life
Knowing we are not alone.

October 6 and 7, 2017

NOTES SCRIBBLED AT THE SAN FRANCISCO BALLET – FEB 13, 1977

What truly is prayer?
The fragility of human life conversing
with the awesome force of the universe?
Tender flesh meeting the shaper of galaxies,
fearlessly and as a friend?
The Cosmic Spirit talking to itself –
Opening one eye –
Briefly knowing itself?

THE AGELESS ONE

There is in you that which is always being born.
The eternal child gazes from your eyes, making
everything he sees fresh and new.
Exciting exploration
Playful wonder
He falls,
cries ALL his tears and rises, undaunted.
He is the lover of life, the knower of secrets, the essence of maturity.
He is the Ageless One.

REVELATION

My joy has burst the bonds of human blindness.
I have known the unknowable but cannot utter it.
I have stepped into the infinite
And seen that we were there already.

It is only our knowing that changes.
In my flesh I have touched the cosmic spirit.

1977

I LIKE BEING OLD

I like being old.
The folly of youth is far behind me.
Undue stress and worry long gone too.
So many lessons hardlearned.
So many scars painfully earned.
(And they were worth it, I tell you.)
As a bone is strong where it broke and knitted,
So it is with my soul.
So many traps I struggled out of.
Many, unknowingly, I built myself.
So many dark nights of the soul,
Steeped in anguish –
Asking – is life worth it?
Then at last the dawn would come
Unforeseeably bright,
A gift of that night,
So now I welcome darkness
And come it always will.
I welcome cherished beliefs broken to pieces,
For I know they are reforming where I cannot see but know I will!
I like being old
Free to marry heart and mind
To create some gift for humankind.
A song rises in me,
A hymn to life so fleeting, yet strong.
I fly on wings that grew when winning
struggles and losing some too!

How liberating to lose and look for the lesson.
No more self-scolding – gratitude instead.
Yes, I have less physical energy,

But I'm not wasting most of it learning how to live.
I use it to live instead.
My own youth was hellish anguish scarcely abated.
My middle years filled with sickness and pain,
The "Pearl Principle" I birthed at age thirteen –
"Turn the painful and ugly into beauty
pristine" – has carried me through.
So now old age is a blessing and benediction.
My candle is shorter, but it burns just as bright.
So dearly I hold it as I walk
Toward endless night.

November 1, 2017
Rewritten September 23, 2021.

TO MY FAITHFUL FORD
WHO SET ME FREE

Ford Escort Wagon,
My driver-friendly, desert-friendly car,
You were cool white and comfy as a mother's arms.
Your embrace said you'd take me far.
Far from home and far from fear,
My lifelong terror of being lost.
Senseless terror taught by a fearful mother.
To be lost is to die she said and told me why.
You gave me courage to face it square.
So I did and named you Dawn Boy.
Blessed you with drum and rattle.
Loved you as a best friend and guide.

Far horizons we faced together.
Never knowing where the night would find us,
Or some howling storm would blind us.
Just you and me and the road.
New Mexico lonely!
Nothing better to teach me trust.
Texas, Oklahoma and Kansas Flint Hills
rolling green like waves of the sea –
all were game for you and me.
Limestone cliffs and scrub oak woodlands beckoned.
Dogwood blossoms and sparkling thousand-fingered lakes
called, and we answered.

We heeded that summons from the heart of childhood,
From the fragrant Ozarks of my native state,
Just you and I, Dawn Boy, headed south by east
And nestled in the arms of piney mountains –
enchanted places where I thought I could never drive.

"Moon-kissed lake by which I stand,
Hidden lake in sheltering forest, hear me.
I have arrived!
I've broken free of crippling fear!"
Lifting my arms, my tear-streaked face
To the Missouri sky, I proclaim –
"I've come home – a child no more!
Rejoice!
Press me to your tender heart.
Embrace me and my staunch companion,
My Dawn Boy who gave me wings to fly.
My faithful Ford who set me free."

July 2010 and Oct. 6, 2021

AND QUIET FLOWS THE RIVER

Slow – slow – slowly
Lift one leg then the other.
Walk down to the river,
To the fabled Rio Grande.

Step down – down – down
Into lifting water
Lifting and fresh – cold – lifting
Calves – thighs – waist – head
Softly the current takes me.

River of dreams, of stories,
Let my story end.
Gently float me
Like crisp weed up from the bottom,
Like a child's sailboat lost to the wind.

Evening skies turn milky blue.
Birdsongs hush to a whisper.
The Black Range engulfs the sun.
And quiet flows the river.

April 28 thru May 9, 1995

TO PHILIP,
A GREEK DANCER AT
EITOS TAVERNA

As a ray of light you come dancing.
As the eternal song you come dancing.
As the laughter of God you come.
Filling us with soft-sung radiance.
Lifting our illusions of mortality.
Lifting the sadness of time.

September 1978
(on a magical night in Berkeley)

THE CHILDREN

Together they gambol up the mountain path,
but each in a different way.
She, delightedly following a butterfly among
the daisies but leaving it free.
He, chasing it, capturing it, jailing it in a jar.

She, reaching out in wonder to sunlit blossoms,
lightly tracing veins in baby-cheek petals
he, reaching out and plucking them –
"How pretty!" he cries, "I'll take them home to Mother."

Together they amble homeward down the path
Each with treasures from the day
His gripped tightly in little boy hands.
Hers held gently in her heart.

MORE THAN ONE MAN

I press you close to my heart and know I hold more than one man.
I hold the history of a people: their torture
and rape – agony – anguish,
Their rage and their war cries, the mother
crying for her dead children,
The widow tearing her hair, chaos,
bewilderment, despair, crushing defeat.
I hold a tale of unspeakable sorrow and undying devotion
A tale of unshakable courage in a hopeless fight.

I press you close and know I hold more than just one man.
I hold the longings of a people that refuse to die, to melt, to blend;
That refuse to forget the beauty and the harmony;
That refuse to forget the sacred circle and the ways of the old ones.
I hold the will of a people to plant the sacred tree
and walk as brothers in love and peace,
the passion of a people to stand straight and proud and free,
The unquenchable fire, the glowing dawn of a new day.
Next to my heart the farseeing eyes of eagle soaring,
The medicine power of wise Grizzly.

DESOLATION

You are gone from our midst!
Leaving us!
To walk an older way.
Emptiness crushes me like a mouse in a vacuum.
The void you leave could contain the universe.
Searing pain in my throat.
Tears that blind me.
Walking as one in shock to the door,
Saying something to my friends – I don't know what.
The black, cold night receives me.
It is over.

DANCING GREEK AT EITOS TAVERNA

Single at last – unfettered – free
Wildly, expansively free.
Coming full flower into womanhood.

1978 and dancing Greek at Eitos Taverna in Berkeley.
Ripe for love – for lust – for adventure.
Swinging hip-length hair over my shoulder
In a shimmering mass of bronze.
Ankle-length skirt split to hip – legs long and shapely.
Feeling my power as Woman –
Exploring it for the first time
A timid little mouse no more.

Our line of dancers winds swaying across the wooden floor
My eyes meeting those of some Greek god
send the message –
"It is you I choose tonight."
Electric sparks between us make his assent
known to me and me alone.

In 1978 I danced to a bouzouki band that
couldn't read music – traditional – pure.
A rare experience I hold dear.
And those Greek gods, if still they live, are ordinary men.
And I was Queen for a moment in time.
Now, I see it clear – this is NOW and that was THEN.

1/19/14 & 2/13/21

MY FOURTH OF JULY, 2015

(In Three Verses)

Fourth of July and I don't need Roman candles
Flinging bright colors across the sky.
I prefer these candles flickering in a room
Holding memories so sweet.
I envision my loved one, my Jeff, doing his slow
ballet to Yanni's ethereal music.
Gracefully he lifts hands upward to the divine,
His upturned face transfigured, sublime.
Then with arms outstretched he wheels serenely
As a bird in flight.
He dances beyond beginnings and endings,
Beyond day and night.

Fourth of July and fireworks boom
in rapid succession overhead,
but they fail to beckon me into the night.
I prefer this music that conjures silence,
and in this winged silence, in this fluttering
amber light, I envision my loved one,
my Jeff, reclining on his seaman's bed –
tender and vulnerable his eyes meet mine.
Kneeling beside him I kiss each cheek,
His forehead, his silken hair
How bright and innocent his eyes are.
I never see one, but two.

I sing him to sleep –
"Arroz Con Pollo" – a children's song in Spanish.
He loves it so.
One last kiss on tender lips
And my dear one melts into slumber.

Fourth of July, yet no need for excitement,
for celebration.
Deeply tranquil in soft-sung light.
Composed.
Complete.
Beyond the sadness of time.

AS EQUALS SHALL WE STAND

The greatest tribute I can give you
is to live my own life in my own way,
with joy and thanksgiving.
The deepest love I can offer you is to love myself
Even as you love yourself
and to put no one ahead of me –
not even you.
As equals shall we stand
In the face of the Cosmic Spirit.

CHICAGO LAKOTA

He was born in the slums of Chicago.
     Born to poverty
     Born to hunger
Orphaned in his own home.
No one to teach him the songs and dances.
No one to tell the sacred stories.
No one to show him Lakota ways.
He went alone to the mountain
     to seek his vision.
He went alone
     and he heard Lakota drums,
     muffled drums from the murky past
     throbbing in the night,
     the ancient songs of his people
     and he heard his heart breaking in answer.
The Chicago Lakota.

He was born in the grime of Chicago
The white man's unspoken rules
     surrounding him like gray smog,
     forever seeping in, stifling him.
A living enemy he would have fought bravely.

But these rules,
These inverted values,
The blindness,
The deafness,
The madness,

Fostered by tradition,
Girded by law,
Backed by guns,
The destruction of everything he held sacred.
How could he fight that?
Slowly they crushed him.
Slowly the fire within went out.
> For he COULD NOT be Indian
> and he WOULD NOT be white.

His spirit stumbled and fell.
His body walked on empty
> through the land that should be his own.
The Chicago Lakota.

May 1, 1973 – Living in East Oakland, CA

SUMMER SOLSTICE ON OCEAN BEACH, SAN FRANCISCO

A True Story of the Summer of Love

Enchanted morning
Cool mist bathes my upturned face.
High above sunlight shimmers on the surface of
This uncanny ceiling of fog.
Cloudless sky overhead – cerulean blue.
Wet sand crisp between my toes.
Beach flecked with stiffened foam,
Glossy white and seeming weightless.
A testimony to lashing waves in the night
But, now in early morn's light,
A looking glass sea.
The world holds its breath anticipating
Something wondrous.
Now, a muffled sound far behind me –
Turning to face it an apparition appears,
Materializes bit by bit from out the fog
A horse – a bay – gleaming, shimmering –
Curried to beyond perfection.
And riding with no bridle – no saddle –
A woman of astounding beauty.
Golden tresses cascade in ripples
From her flower-wreathed head –
Ripples glinting needles of silver light.
Her gauzy raiment in shades of pearly gray and white
Floats gossamer-like as befits a fairy queen

Her neck and breast bedecked with leis
Of brilliant flowers,
Bedecked, also, her bay with lush blossoms –
Red, white, pink, yellow and blue.
Stately he walks knowing he bears a queen.

From the fog more equine beauty emerges,
In single file they come, making a grand entrance each one.
Chestnut, black, white, and dappled gray.
The sheen of their coats incredible.
All free of saddles and bridles.
All draped with multi-colored leis.
All mounted by youth – men and women of glowing
Countenance and royal demeanor.
Perfect control of horses,
Though no word is spoken.
Serenely they step into the water
Which mirrors them complete.
Hooves making ripples which soon disappear.
Gracefully as in ballet the riders cast their
Leis onto the water where they linger and float.
The dance continues as the royal equines
Gently wheel and return to land.
By ones, twos, and threes they melt into the mist
Leaving me awash in wonder.
I fall to my knees in the sand,
Pressing hands to heart, I burst into tears.
How else to respond to awesome beauty.
A marvel beyond my ability or will to explain.
Let the mystery remain.

OKLAHOMA FROM THE
MIDNIGHT TRAIN (1956)

My mind returns dreamlike to that little wooden car
with wooden benches and red paint peeling.
Returns to the swing and sway
The soft clickity-clack
Of train wheels on moon-silvered track.

A lullaby of rhythm on a full moon night.
Once again through the open window
A warm breeze brushes my face
And it's redolent with the loamy scent of fields –
The corn, the wheat, the alfalfa
I see shimmering ponds, windmills, and oil wells
Soaring upward resplendent and strong

I see scattered stands of trees
Cradling sleeping farm houses.
Dreamily the train rolls through vast stretches of prairie
With herds of cattle, sheep and hogs
With haystacks, corncribs, silos,
weathered barns and fences.
All glistening in the moonlit night.
All swept clean with the vast wind,

PRECIOUS MAN SO FAR FROM ME

Wanting you, always wanting you and the wanting my brightest joy,
my sweetest sorrow.
Dear man half my age, never could you be
drawn to me as I am drawn to you.
Longing now to press cheek to cheek and
melt into you like a little white cloud into sunshine.
What paradox is this?
That first second I loved you
I was transformed by a burst of Cosmic Joy.
Stood grounded and centered in my power.
Young again in body, soul, and mind.
Renewed courage, creativity, and drive to help all mankind.
This unrequited love,
This sacred love through which I have new life also wounds.
And this wounding I will treasure in equal measure with my love
for sorrow and joy are the twin faces of life.

April 30, 2021

MY MAN OF THE NORTHWOODS

On the moon-silvered lake
we sit in your birchbark canoe.
How handsome you are, my Ojibway,
my man of shimmering lights.
How fine you look with moonlight gleaming
from smoothly brushed and braided long black hair.
Rivaling the sheen from silver around your neck,
your wrists and fingers,
and moon-round hair ties glowing,
Glinting needles of snow-toned light.
Your bronze-hued face reflects in still waters
On this luminous night.

Oh, my man of the North,
of the icy wind blowing and tree-popping nights.
My man of the frozen lakes
and whispering snow in the pines.
Brave bow hunter of ice-heavy forests.
Man of the mysterious Northern Lights.
How intriguing you are, adorned in desert silver.
How gently resplendent in the riches of my canyon people.
You enchant me.
You with starlight eyes and a hearth-warm smile.
Strong quiet man in moon-drenched silver.
My man of softly shimmering lights.

MARCH 25, 1994

Outside my window junipers bob and thrash
Their nesting songbirds fall suddenly silent.
Sun Valley Trailers button down tight
Against swirling dust
Lashing them whiplike.
The TV antenna moans and creaks
Like the rigging of a tall ship.
And that bony feral cat huddles, blinking
Under the porch of the abandoned house.

PAEAN TO THE MENSES

I recall the upwelling love for all humanity my menses engendered.
My heart opened wide, embracing all.
Tenderness
A desire to heal wounds.
To listen to cries of the bereaved, the abandoned
A desire to understand the misunderstood.

As my life's blood flowed so my compassion flowed.
Folding the lost in loving arms,
Making them found – making them whole.
I recall feeling one with warming Sun.
One with mellow moon soothing anguished spirits.
One with cooling night caressing fevered brows,
Whispering "peace" into the ears of those who fear and fret
Holding the hands of those who walk alone,
but long for companions.

I recall as my menses flowed feeling my kinship with Mother Earth.
Fecund with creativity welling up.
Fecund with aspiration to heal hearts
sealed by fear of further wounding.
Fecund with longing to bring love of living

To the weary, the depressed.
Oh, the richness – the exuberant tenderness –
The robust yet lyric blossoming of
womanhood – the monthly magic.

December 7, 2013

MY HEART CANNOT LET GO

My heart cannot let go.
I relish gazing at his picture on the mantle,
This timeless photo of the man I long to know.
Yes, eleven years married and still longing.
Too late! I cry. Too late!
His ashes grace the mantle – let him go!
And yet, as never before, I feel his presence in this image –

His living, breathing presence.
On the Deming desert he stands as though rooted
in the sand where he belongs as surely as prickly pear and sage.
Wind lifts a lock of his silken hair,
Shimmering dark hair against Deming blue.
Tenderly it caresses him as I was wont to do,
How resolute that man, unflappable.

Hands on hips, exuding vitality, yet relaxed.
Purposeful, confident, commanding.
Strong in body, in will, virile alpha male.
My man-to-be in a distant future.
No! Not mine! Not anyone's! Not ever!
Always just out of reach,
Enticing, unknowable man.

What happened, I cry to the uncaring void?
What happened to so change him before his coming to me?
Why only glimpses of what he used to be?
But they drew me in – bit by bit – those glimpses.

My heart caught fire with passion, with adoration, with hope –
would he open like a flower?
I tell you – that once-hidden man lives
and breathes in this very photo.
It's all I have left, more than I had before!
How can I consign him to an album in some dark desk drawer?

June 7, 2020 Sunday

For his memorial at the Black Cat 6/14/20 Sunday
He died March 1, 2020 at 11:06 a.m. Sunday

CABALLO LAKE STATE PARK –
MID-AUGUST '07

High noon and stillness
Profound stillness – magical – unreal.
Nothing moves save me.
Delicate tamarisks immobile.
Fern-like mesquites immobile.
No leaf stirs in the cottonwood's
topmost branches.
While the Rio's smooth face reflects
Red cliffs and puffball clouds
Dazzling white and unchanging
as though painted.
No shadows anywhere.
The whole earth suffused with brilliance.
It permeates my every pore
I breathe it in.
A paradox of peace and exhilaration
fills the air – fills me.
I lift my arms to the heavens with
a sense of soaring – expanding –
becoming boundless.

NOT WITH MY NEED

It is not with my need that I love you,
But with my fullness to overflowing.
When I am filled with happiness or with bitter tears
I will come to you that we might share them.
But I will not ask you to fill my emptiness.
For that, I must drink from the Great Source directly;
Even as you must drink – directly and alone.

POEM BASED ON A JUNE 26, 1991
STREAM OF CONSCIOUSNESS

Kittery, Maine

From the depths,
The unfathomed depths,
The ocean washes up shells
wet and gleaming on tawny sand.
Pale suns blushing on some.
Desert colors on others,
Pearlescent rainbows spread around me.

Now words – words washing up from the depths, like shells
Surprises!
Fragile surprises that I sort,
Arrange into patterns or return to the sea within

Each high tide leaves its offering.
Storms churn – dig deep – offer up
strange and broken pieces.
Forms I cannot quite discern yet trigger
things half-forgotten – a whisper –
a ghost from the past.
Oh! strange and lovely pieces,
Bizarre, broken pieces
I touch you with timid fingers
Arrange and rearrange you
Still trying to complete the pattern in the gray dawn.

WHATEVER

I haven't written a pity poem in 63 years.
Yet, like the rising tide, I feel one coming on.
So, if you don't wanna hear one more "life's a bitch" poem,
better close your ears,
'Cause this little ditty – this rueful bit of useless
pity is headed for darkness not for dawn.

I kept waking at 3 a.m.,
A huge void inside or so it seemed at first,
A total lack of anything to say –
Emptiness – zilch – no hunger – no thirst.
Not the faintest longing for light – for day.
All this in the spiritual way.

But the emptiness did not stay.
First impressions can be so mistaken.
It's not a lack of something to say;
it's the feelings I'd forsaken.
It's fear, anger, grief, love, delusion,
Right-wrong, stop-go, friend or foe confusion.
It's tilting all windmills at once.
It's riding, hell-bent, in all directions, no pausing, no reflection.

Taking all paths at once equals paralysis –
A wildly energized paralysis exploding like a used-up star.
Black hole forming,
sucking in all thought, all hope, all need.
Yet through its wormy wormhole it spits out this ditty –
This sorry little poem of naked self-pity.

January 10-12, 2019

SO RADIANT YOUR HUMOR

For a man so strong, so virile,
Your laughter is intriguing.
It is soft, like the sounds of your Northern Woods
Liquid like the sound of water.
And the laughter of your laughter endears you to me.
It is silent as the Northern Lights,
And as gently radiant.
In hushed mystery it shimmers across your
face, filling the night with color.
I long to touch that mystery,
Tenderly,
Cautiously,
To feel it tingle in my fingers,
I yearn to feel God's humor in the contours of your face.

SOMEDAY

On this ridge I stand,
The broad desert spread before me.
My heart weeping tears of joy,
I radiate love like sunshine
stroking this land,
Hungering to draw it in to me –
to meld as one.

Nearby a friendly breeze lifts the sand,
swirls it 'round and 'round
making it shimmer in the morning sun
Then drops it 'neath a palo verde tree
And I think, someday that will be me.

Someday, I'll be blowing in the wind.
I'll be motes of dust in a sunbeam
delighting some child as they once delighted me.
I'll be snowflakes drifting down to spread
a blanket of white and coat every tree.
A world of magic for all to see.

Someday, I'll be specks of dust that raindrops
Form around and fall in silvery streaks to the ground
Bringing life to every thirsty plant
Flooding the nest of some poor ant,

Over there a cactus flower – pink – hugging the ground.
Someday in that I will be found.

Then Turtle will come along
and happily munch me down
then bask dreaming in the sun.

On this ridge I stand
The vast desert spread before me.
Knowing I'm a part of everything.
and ever will be.
Even coyote loping far below.

Him and his scat.
I'll be part even of that.
The lovely and the ugly.
The sweet and the foul.
Is it so different now?

PREMONITIONS

Now come premonitions too young to share
Too tender to tell
The shape of things to come
Forms in fine mist so tenuous
I dare not touch it lest I alter the shape.
Nor dare I lend it my breath
Lest it dissipate.

So gently hold the hope.
So warmly nurse the dream.
So softly tiptoe toward the future.